P9-BZG-088

PENGUIN WORKSHOP
An Imprint of Penguin Random House LLC, New York

Penguin supports copyright. Copyright fuels creativity, encourages diverse voices, promotes free speech, and creates a vibrant culture. Thank you for buying an authorized edition of this book and for complying with copyright laws by not reproducing, scanning, or distributing any part of it in any form without permission. You are supporting writers and allowing Penguin to continue to publish books for every reader.

The publisher does not have any control over and does not assume any responsibility for author or third-party websites or their content.

Copyright © 2020 by Sky Brown, Inc. All rights reserved.
Published by Penguin Workshop, an imprint of Penguin Random House LLC, New York.
PENGUIN and PENGUIN WORKSHOP are trademarks of Penguin Books Ltd,
and the W colophon is a registered trademark of Penguin Random House LLC.
Manufactured in China.

Visit us online at www.penguinrandomhouse.com.

Library of Congress Cataloging-in-Publication Data is available upon request.

ISBN 9780593096970
1 3 5 7 9 10 8 6 4 2

SKY
BROWN

SKY'S THE LIMIT
WORDS OF WISDOM FROM
A YOUNG CHAMPION

Penguin Workshop

My name is
SKY BROWN.

I first started skateboarding and surfing
when I was two or three. I may still be little, but
when I'm skateboarding and surfing, I feel like

I CAN BE ME,
that
I CAN BE STRONG,
and that
NOBODY CAN STOP ME.

Sometimes I'm afraid to fall.
If you feel like you're going to fall,

YOU'RE GOING TO FALL.

But if you don't think you're going to fall, you're not going to fall. It's an exciting feeling, knowing you are

PUSHING YOUR LIMITS and CHALLENGING YOURSELF.

My motto is:
BE BRAVE,
BE STRONG,
HAVE FUN,
and do it because
YOU LOVE IT!

YOU CAN DO ANYTHING,

even if you're scared. I was scared to try dancing, but I got that excited feeling that I get when I dare myself to do a new trick, or try something new. It was

100% WORTH THE RISK.

The most important thing is to
HAVE FUN
and to
TRY YOUR BEST.

There are a lot of things

I CAN DO.

There are a lot of things

I WANT TO DO.

Whatever it is, I do it with

LOVE AND HAPPINESS.

When people say I'm not good enough,

I WANT TO PROVE THEM WRONG.

I give it everything to show them that

I *CAN* DO IT.

MY BROTHER IS MY BEST FRIEND.

We push each other in skateboarding and surfing, but at the end of the day I know

HE ALWAYS HAS MY BACK.

I love him for always being by my side and supporting me.

My goal is to

BUILD CONFIDENCE

in all girls around the world by inspiring
them and showing them that we can
take on any kind of challenge.

**SKY'S THE
LIMIT.**

GIRLS CAN DO
ANYTHING
BOYS CAN DO!

Don't let anyone convince you otherwise.

My secret little tip?

DON'T FEEL PRESSURE, JUST HAVE FUN!

If you're not having fun, you're forgetting why you started in the first place.

It doesn't matter if you're
**A BOY OR GIRL,
BIG OR SMALL,
YOUNG OR OLD . . .**
you can do
ANYTHING!